DATE DUE		

The Treasure of Inheritance

by Roy A. Gallant

BENCHMARK BOOKS

MARSHALL CAVENDISH
NEW YORK

Series Editor: Roy A. Gallant

Series Consultants:

LIFE SCIENCES
Dr. Edward J. Kormondy
Chancellor and Professor of Biology (retired)
University of Hawaii-Hilo/West Oahu

PHYSICAL SCIENCES
Dr. Jerry LaSala
Department of Physics
University of Southern Maine

Benchmark Books
Marshall Cavendish
99 White Plains Road
Tarrytown, NY 10591-9001

Library of Congress Cataloging-in-Publication Data
Gallant, Roy A.
      The treasure of inheritance / by Roy A. Gallant
            p. cm.—(The story of science)
Includes bibliographical references and index.
Summary: Discusses how living things inherit traits, chronicles the history of the study of heredity, and examines current research on genetic engineering and the mapping of the human gene.
ISBN 0-7614-1426-6
      1. Genetics-Juvenile literature. 2. Heredity-Juvenile literature. [1. Genetics. 2. Heredity.]
      I. Title. II. Series.
QH437.5 .G35   2002   576.5-dc21   200200010

Photo Research by Linda Sykes Picture Research, Hilton Head, SC
Diagrams by Ian Warpole on pages: 18, 20, 29, 30, 33, 34, 35, 36, 39, 44, 48
Cover: Roy A. Gallant
Photo Credits: Peter Menzel/Stock Boston: 1; Stephen Krasemann/Photo Researchers, Inc.: 7 (bottom); Nigel Dennis/Photo Researchers, Inc.: 7 (top left); Julie Habel/Corbis: 7 (top right); Mark Edwards/Still Pictures/Peter Arnold, Inc.: 8; Ken Garrett/National Geographic Image Sales: 9; Charles and Josette Lenars/Corbis: 10–11; Mark Burnett/Stock Boston: 13; Robert Dowling/Corbis: 14 (left); Peter Chadwick/Science Photo Library/Photo Researchers, Inc.: 14 (right); Dr. Jeremy Burgess/Science Photo Library/Photo Researchers, Inc.: 17 (left); Biophoto Associates/Photo Researchers, Inc.: 17 (right), 20–21; 35 (bottom); Bo Weisland/MI&I/Science Photo Library/Photo Researchers, Inc.: 20; CNRI/Science Photo Library/ Photo Researchers, Inc.: 22–23; Prof. P. Motta/Dept. of Anatomy/University La Sapienza, Rome/Photo Researchers, Inc.: 24; Francis Leroy, Biocosmos/Science Photo Library/Photo Researchers, Inc.: 25; Andrew Martinez/ Photo Researchers, Inc.: 26; Archive/Photo Researchers, Inc.: 27; Science Photo Library/Photo Researchers, Inc.: 28, 67; Andrew Syred/Science Photo Library/Photo Researchers, Inc.: 38; Photo Researchers, Inc.: 40; The Royal Collection © HM Queen Elizabeth II: 41; Frans Lanting/Minden Pictures: 43; Corbis: 45; A. Barrington Brown/Photo Researchers, Inc.: 46; Meckes/Ottawa/Photo Researchers, Inc.: 50–51; Archivio Iconografico, S.A./Corbis: 51; Reunion des Musees Nationaux/Art Resource NY: 52; AP/Wide World Photos: 54; Nathaniel H. Robin, M.D., Associate Professor of Genetics and Pediatrics, Center for Human Genetics, Case Western Reserve University/University Hospitals of Cleveland: 57; © Rob Lewine photography/Corbis: 58; Najlah Feanny/Stock Boston: 61; TimePix: 62–63; Jeanne White/Photo Researchers, Inc.: 66; R. Van Nostrand/Photo Researchers, Inc.: 66 (right); Bruno Zehnder/Peter Arnold, Inc.: 68; James King-Holmes/Photo Researchers, Inc.: 70–71.

Cover design by Bob O'Brien

Printed in Hong Kong
6 5 4 3 2 1

For My Grandchildren

Contents

One

Seeds and Monsters

Perhaps the most remarkable thing about all creatures is their ability to make copies of themselves. That magic of nature has maintained an unbroken chain of life for nearly four billion years. Although all human beings closely resemble one another, some telling differences distinguish one group, and one individual, from another.

You have probably noticed that people with fair skin color often have blue eyes and blond hair. The two somehow go together. They also tend to have thin lips and high-bridged noses. As a group these people look different from people whose skin, hair, and other features are darker in color. Each individual within each group shares a chemical blueprint that accounts for the general appearance of the group, or the

The magic of inheritance works in many ways. One of the most obvious is the resemblance of offspring to their parents, whether those parents are humans, as on this book's front cover, foxes, cats, or even hippopotami.

sameness of certain group features. The sameness among individuals becomes increasingly evident at the family level, and most evident in identical twins.

Biologists have discovered these chemical blueprints and learned how to read them over the last 150 years. Their study is called *heredity*, and the science underlying that study is called *genetics*. It did not spring up overnight but evolved gradually over many centuries. Several thousand years ago the ancient Babylonians and Egyptians practiced crossbreeding of food crops to make them grow faster and stronger. Such

Even 10,000 years ago, farmers learned to produce high yield crops by cross-breeding plants through trial and error. Here, Burkina Faso men cut sorghum plants while women gather the seeds.

During ancient times when wild cattle were being tamed for farm use, cows would not give up their milk unless their calves were nearby. This ancient Egyptian farmer holds a calf near its mother while another farmer does the milking.

knowledge came slowly over many years, with some experiments working better than others. Around 10,000 years ago native peoples of Central and South America learned how to combine different types of maize, or corn, to produce especially strong plants with large ears. Other peoples used controlled breeding to domesticate wild animals and then improve their usefulness to man. The ancient Babylonians left stone carvings that show calves tied to the necks of their mothers. The cattle were still partly wild and would give milk only when stimulated in the presence of their calves. Over time, only gentle cows were selected for breeding, until dairy cows like those of today gave their milk willingly, without needing their calves to be there. If you compare the size of hen's eggs marketed in Western countries with the very small eggs laid by the wilder hens kept by tribal peoples, you will quickly realize the advantage of careful and selective breeding.

Aristotle and Dragon's Teeth

Even though people in ancient times learned how to grow a better garden or breed a calmer cow, they did not know the rules of inheritance and so did not understand the biological magic they were working. It wasn't until the golden age of the ancient Greek thinkers, which began around 500 B.C., that questions and theories about inheritance began to be considered. Among those early thinkers was the philosopher Aristotle, who lived from 384 to 322 B.C. By his time, people understood that newborn humans and many other animal species were produced by a male and a female having sex together. They also understood that offspring could be produced only between a male and female of the same species, and that the two parents in some unknown way contributed to the appearance and behavior of the offspring.

Mythical beings—part-human, part-beast—were imagined by the ancient Egyptians and Babylonians to have superhuman powers and strength. The great Egyptian sphinx, part-lion and part-man, symbolized the pharoah's power.

If you knew those three things, you knew all that was then known about human reproduction and heredity.

Aristotle rejected many superstitions of his time: that the weasel gave birth to its young through the ear, that ravens had sex with their beaks, and that armed men sprang up where dragon's teeth had been planted by the biblical Jason. On the other hand he believed in *spontaneous generation*—that living matter sprang forth from nonliving matter. He said that worms and other creatures were made from the soil, that mosquitoes and fleas were generated out of decaying matter, and that the morning dew gave rise to fireflies. Such beliefs lasted for more than a thousand years.

One of Aristotle's main interests in heredity was just how much each parent contributed to the traits of his or her offspring. He suspected, incorrectly, that the female contributed more than the male. No one at the time knew why an infant might be born a boy or a girl. Aristotle thought that gender might be determined by the degree of heat in the mother's womb. He and others at that time spoke of the union of a male seed and a female seed in reproduction. They believed that those seeds contained everything a child was to become—the way he or she would look and behave. Today, those "seeds" are called eggs in females and sperm in males. The philosopher Anaxagoras, who lived from 500 to 428 B.C., thought that an infant's gender was determined by the male seed, an offspring born from a seed of the male parent's right testis being male and a seed from the left testis producing a female. If a child looked more like its mother than its father, it was said that the mother's seed "prevailed," or was the stronger.

Aristotle further believed that parents passed on to their children not only inborn physical characteristics such as hair

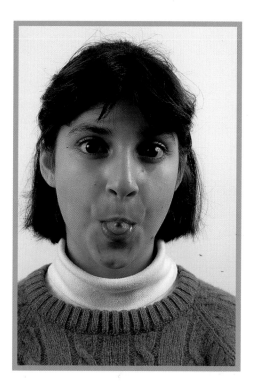

Can you roll your tongue like this? Seven out of ten people can. It is an inherited ability controlled by a dominant gene. Some people can even do an upside-down tongue roll.

and eye color, but *acquired characteristics* as well, such as the habit of telling lies, stealing, or a lost finger resulting from an accident. A criminal, for instance, would pass on to his children his leaning toward crime. Some carried that idea to the extreme by saying that a child could inherit a parent's criminal behavior even if the child were born before the parent ever committed a crime. But, as it turns out, acquired characteristics are not inherited. Lambs have their tails cut off when they are born, so each lamb's short tail is an acquired characteristic. Although lambs have had their tails clipped off for more than a hundred generations, they continue to be born with long tails. The acquired characteristic of a short tail is never passed on through heredity. And well-groomed poodle parents do not give birth to fancy-looking poodle pups.

If this fancy-cut poodle gave rise to a thousand offspring, not one would inherit its parent's high-fashion coat because it was acquired by trimming. Offspring of the leopard, however, will inherit its parent's spots since the markings are not acquired, but passed down through the genes.

Seeds and Pangenesis

But Aristotle correctly thought that children could be like their distant ancestors. As evidence he cited a white woman who had a daughter by a black man. Although the daughter was white, the son of the daughter was black. The rules of heredity that govern the reappearance of certain family traits, such as skin or eye color, were not discovered until the mid-1800s.

The famous Greek physician Hippocrates, who was born around 460 B.C., thought that all parts of the body contributed one or more aspects to heredity. All were then collected in the male and female "seed." A seed, then, contained a blueprint of each parent's body part, a notion called pangenesis. Sometimes, however, a blueprint was not followed exactly and terrible things were wrong in a newborn. A child might be mentally retarded or born with extra limbs or no arms. People believed that angry gods would show their displeasure by causing children to be born with imperfections. The most severely deformed infants were sometimes left in the wilderness to die.

It would be many centuries before the magical and superstitious beliefs about heredity would be replaced by scientific understanding. This was made possible by new attitudes and a marvelous new instrument, the microscope.

Two

Microscopes, Gemmules, and Peas

The problem of heredity became much easier to tackle beginning in 1665 when the English scientist Robert Hooke put his homemade microscopes to work. Although the microscopes of Hooke's time magnified things up to only 100 to 200 times, they still opened a whole new world that had previously been invisible. Later microscopes were able to magnify things thousands of times.

The microscope of the brilliant English scientist Robert Hooke (1635–1703) is shown here with a flame shining through a lens as a source of light. His many drawings, such as one revealing the compound eye of a blue fly, showed many details never before observed in nature.

Battle between Egg and Sperm

It remained for the uneducated Dutch genius Antonie van Leeuwenhoek, who lived from 1632 to 1723, to make more powerful microscopes and see that new world in even more fascinating detail. He made more than 270 microscopes, grinding his own tiny lenses. He studied pond water, sand fleas, lice, and all

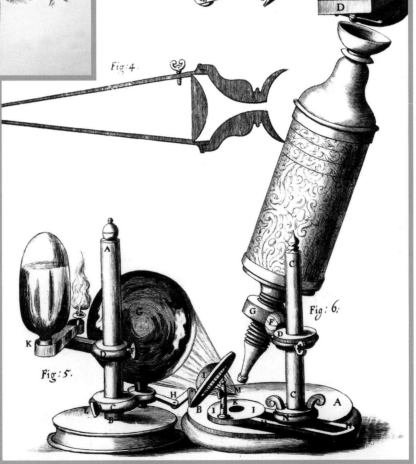

sorts of food particles scraped from between his teeth. Some five years before Leeuwenhoek began to explore his microscopic world, a fellow Dutchman named Régnier de Gräfe made a momentous discovery. He learned that the female organ called an *ovary* released an egglike particle that journeyed through a tube from the ovary down into the womb. There it grew into a new human being, but not on its own. Its development, de Gräfe concluded, required the presence of the male sex fluid called semen. De Gräfe's discovery was greeted with much enthusiasm and gave rise to a group called ovists, after the Latin word *ovum,* meaning egg. Here, they thought, was proof of Aristotle's teaching that the female contributed most to the creation of new offspring. "Why should not the egg," they asked, "contain within it the sole and universal principle of heredity in all life?"

In only a few short years Leeuwenhoek was to make a second major discovery. On examining the semen of several animals, including that of human males, he was astonished to find that the semen

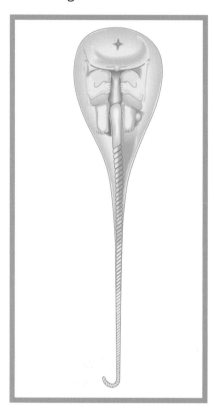

The false notion that human beings developed directly from sperm cells came from Antonie van Leeuwenhoek, who claimed to have seen a miniature person inside the head of a sperm cell. The improbable tiny creature was called a homunculus.

was not a clear fluid but contained tiny tailed creatures swimming about like tadpoles but with heads only one-ten-thousandth of an inch across. He had discovered *sperm*, or the male sex cell counterpart of the female egg sex cell. Leeuwenhoek became convinced that human beings develop from the sperm rather than from the egg because he claimed to see a tiny version of a human being within a single sperm head. We know now that the notion of such a diminutive human being—called a *homunculus*—was nonsense, but Leeuwenhoek and his followers believed it. They came to be known as spermists. They also believed that the function of a woman's womb was only to protect and nourish the homunculus until it was born.

Ovists and spermists alike believed that humans were preformed as miniature versions of an adult and were packaged either in the egg or sperm. Rather than immediately leading to enlightenment, the microscope brewed a storm of hereditary squabbles between the ovists and spermists. But the question remained: Did the real stuff of heredity come from the egg or the sperm? Or maybe from both?

Cells, Eggs, and Sperm

About two billion sperm packed together would fit into the space of half a pencil eraser. The same number of human egg cells would fit easily in a teaspoon. Yet these two tiny structures contain everything needed to produce a person who grows up to be a 330-pound linebacker or a 160-pound Einstein.

Before the significance, complexity, and potential of human eggs and sperm could be understood, biologists first had to unravel the secrets of cells, which are the basic units of life. By the mid-1800s two German biologists, Theodor Schwann and Matthias Schleiden, realized that all living things, including moths, pine trees, and people, are made of cells. Most cells are much smaller than the dot over this letter i. Yet the tiniest cell is able to carry out all of the basic life functions, and that is why a single cell is such a remarkable thing. It feeds, rids itself of waste matter, grows, repairs its damaged parts, and produces more cells just like itself. Your body is made up of some 10 quadrillion (10,000,000,000,000,000) cells of about a hundred different kinds. The cells of your bone marrow start out as generalized cells that can change into specialized ones that become organized as your liver, lungs, kidneys, and other body parts.

Our reproductive cells—egg cells and sperm cells—are highly specialized. A male's sperm cells are produced continuously throughout the male's adult life in two glands called the *testes*. When a

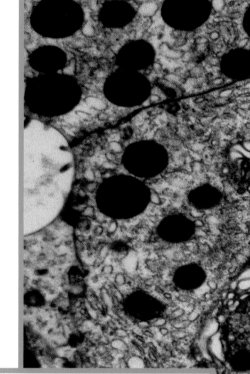

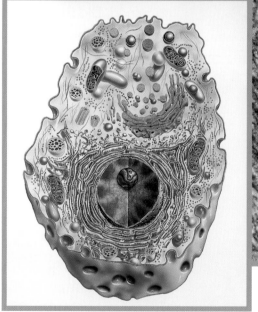

The photomicrograph (far right) shows an animal (rat) cell magnified 1,875 times its actual size. Both the micrograph and the drawing clearly show the large cell nucleus, which is the command center of cells.

Surrounding the nucleus are many other cell structures, each playing special roles in maintaining the cell's various functions.

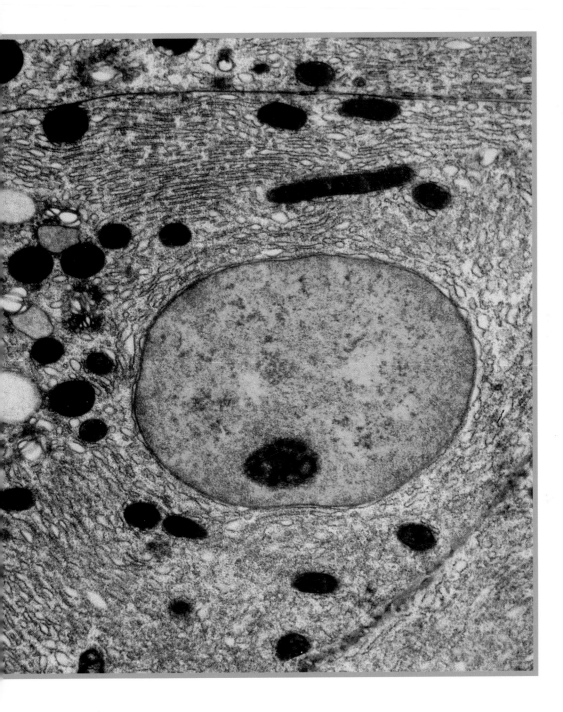

male is sexually aroused, huge numbers of sperm cells—up to about 350 million—mix with a thick fluid that becomes the semen. The semen is then expelled from the body through the penis. The sperm cell has an oval head inside of which is the cell *nucleus*, or control center, for all of the cell's activities. A long tail lashes from side to side, enabling the cell, once injected into a female, to swim about in search of an egg. A typical sperm cell has a useful life of about twenty-four hours before it dies.

The female egg cell is many times larger than a sperm cell. Even so, it is barely visible without a microscope. It is a sac of fluid called *cytoplasm* enclosed with a thick membrane. A large nucleus surrounded by fat droplets of yolk give the cell a grainlike appearance. At birth a human female has up to about 500,000 egg cells, but only about 400 will be released during her child-bearing years. A female typically releases one egg every twenty-eight days. Once freed from an ovary, the egg is swept down through a special tube leading to the womb. If sperm cells are present in the tube, they all attempt to penetrate the egg, but only one manages to do so. The useful life of a human egg is only

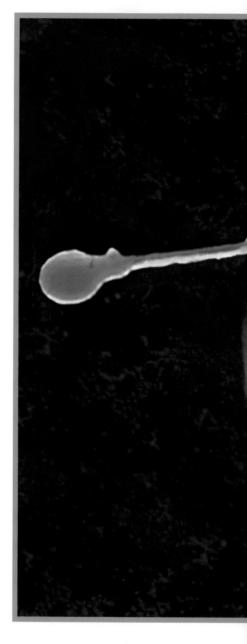

a few hours. The fusion of a sperm cell with an egg cell is called *fertilization*. Once an egg cell has been fertilized it completes its journey down into the womb where it burrows into the soft tissue of the

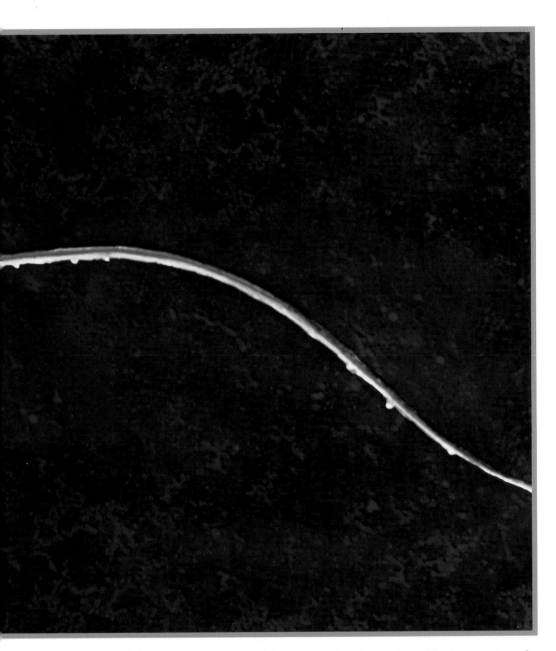

A human male sperm cell, here magnified 1,700 times life size, consists of a head, neck, and tail region. The head contains the genetic material and cell nucleus needed to fertilize the female egg cell. The tail propels the sperm cell toward the egg cell with whiplash movements.

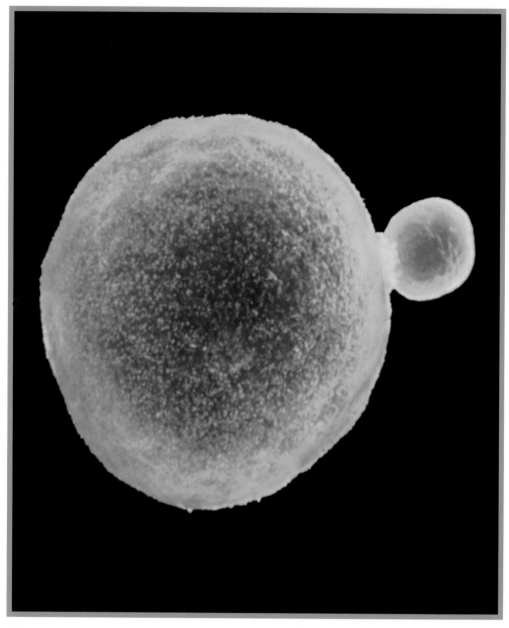

A human female egg cell (green) here magnified 700 times life size. The smaller yellow attachment, called a polar body, later degenerates. The formation of polar bodies is part of the egg cell's development into a mature ovum.

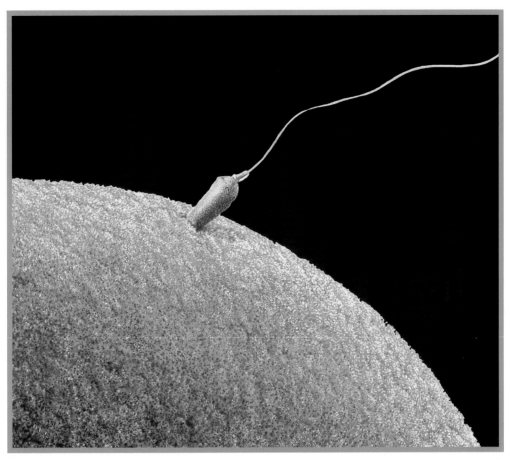

In the act of fertilization, the male sperm cell penetrates the female egg cell by first forcing its way through an outer layer of protective smaller cells, and then through the egg cell membrane. After poking through the egg cell membrane, the sperm cell fuses with the ovum cell nucleus in the act of fertilization.

wall. There it will remain for about nine months, being nourished by the mother's body fluids and gradually developing into a fetus. At the end of nine months, it is expelled through the birth canal as an infant. If the whole process has gone well, the infant is normal and healthy, but so many things can go wrong that scientists still marvel that deformed and otherwise abnormal babies are the exception and not the rule.

The fertilization process was first closely observed in sea urchins, the eggs of which are fertilized by sperm cells outside the animal's body.

Sexual reproduction is the fusion of a female egg sex cell with a male sperm sex cell, both cells being called *gametes*. And it occurs the same way in baboons, elephants, whales, rose bushes, fir trees, and humans. When the egg and sperm nuclei unite, a new life begins.

English naturalist Charles Darwin imagined that the body had physical particles, which he called gemmules, that determined eye and hair color and other traits. Today we call those particles genes.

Darwin and Mendel

By the mid-to-late 1800s scientists had come to know about the activities of sperm and egg cells, but the exact hereditary role of each during fertilization was still unknown. One of the scientists puzzled by the mystery of heredity was the English naturalist Charles Darwin, whose book, *On the Origin of Species by Means of Natural Selection*, was published in 1859. The most important book on biology ever written, it explained in great detail how some species of animals and plants become extinct and how new species come into being through the process of evolution.

But one piece of the puzzle he could not find was how heredity worked. He rejected one theory called *blending inheritance*, which stated that if an animal with black fur mated with a similar animal with white fur, all of the offspring would have gray fur. The original black-fur and white-fur traits would be lost because, once blended, the two traits could never be separated again. His reason for rejecting that idea was that when pigeons, livestock, and plants were bred, the original trait always reappeared in later generations. Instead, Darwin turned to a version of Hippocrates's theory of pangenesis. He imagined that each trait, including eye color, tallness, and skin color, was associated with particles that he called gemmules. They branched off from the body's tissues and collected in egg and sperm cells where they waited to be assembled in a newly fertilized cell, called a *zygote*. Although few went along with Darwin's gemmules, his theory echoed throughout the rest of the century. It reinforced the notion that hereditary traits were real physical particles that went by a variety of other names, including ids, biophores, and pangenes. Today we call them genes.

Before Darwin died in 1882, but unknown to him, the mystery of heredity was being solved by an Austrian monk and plant breeder named Gregor Mendel, who lived across the English Channel in Moravia from 1822 to 1884. After failing his teacher's exams in natural history, Mendel was so discouraged that he gave up his scientific work. He turned to studying the weather, breeding mice, observing bees, and growing vegetables. It was through this last activity that he gained fame as a scientist, but only after his death. Mendel's work was published only six years after Darwin's great book, but it went unnoticed for forty years.

By breeding pea plants, Mendel discovered two major rules in the way heredity works. All of his experimental plants were of the same species but quite different in appearance. Some were tall, others short; some had yellow seeds, others green; some had wrinkled seeds, others round. Also, the plants with red flowers always produced offspring with red flowers when both parent plants had red flowers. Likewise, tall plants always produced other tall plants, and so on with other traits, which are called *phenotypes*. In all, Mendel worked with thirty-four pea plant types that always *bred true*, which means they produced offspring just like themselves. Each type, Mendel reasoned, must be controlled by some substance that he called a "factor." So here was still another term to add to the list—ids, gemmules, particles, biophores, pangenes, and now, factors.

Austrian botanist-monk Gregor Mendel's work with pea plants in the 1800s enabled him to discover two major rules that showed how heredity works. Although Mendel lived during Darwin's time, the two great men never met.

The Rule of Dominance

Mendel next bred two plants that differed in only one trait, or phenotype—height, for instance. When he crossed a pure-bred tall plant with a pure-bred short plant, all the offspring were tall. Clearly, this showed that the idea of blending inheritance was false; otherwise all of the offspring would have been medium height, not tall. This told Mendel that the hereditary particles in the sex cell that controlled tallness in some way overpowered the particles in the other plant's sex cell that controlled shortness. So the particles for the tallness phenotype were said to be *dominant*, which we can write as (T) and those for shortness were said to be recessive, or (t).

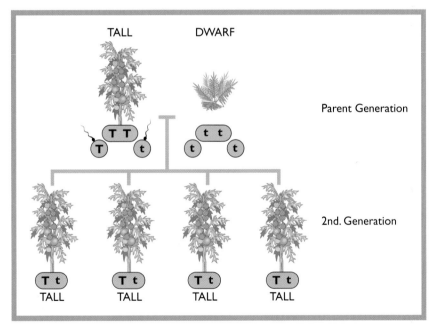

When Mendel crossed tall (T) parent pea plants with short (t) parent pea plants, all members of the next generation were tall (T). This was so because the tallness trait was dominant over the shortness trait. Even though each second-generation plant had one gene for tallness (T) and one for shortness (t), all the plants were tall.

So far so good, but Mendel had a question. What happened to the particles that controlled shortness when the two plants were crossbred? Did they just disappear and not show up in the gametes of the offspring? Or were they there, but just not doing anything?

The Rule of Segregation

Mendel solved the puzzle of the disappearing trait of short-ness when he allowed two of the offspring tall plants to pro-duce a third generation by using their own sperm-cell (pollen) and egg-cell gametes. The results were three tall plants and

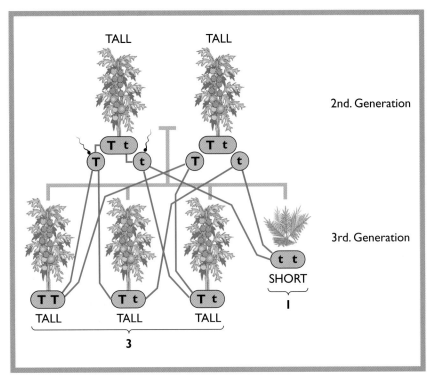

When Mendel crossed two second-generation pea plants, each with one gene for tallness (T) and one for shortness (t), the results were three tall plants to one short plant. The single third-generation short plant was short because it lacked a dominant (T) gene for tallness, whereas each of the other plants had one.

one short. So the heredity factor for shortness wasn't lost at all, it just didn't get expressed in the second generation. Instead it popped up in the third generation in a ratio of three talls to one short. There could be no mistake. Of the 1,064 second-generation plants he bred, 787 of them were tall and 277 were short, a ratio of three to one. Further, the same ratio proved true for the thousands of plants he bred for the other traits of seed color, seed roughness, flower color, and so on. Since these recessive traits were never lost, Mendel reasoned that each parent plant must have two heredity factors for each trait, but that whenever a sex-cell gamete is formed it receives only one factor. In the case of tall/short plants, a sex cell would receive either the factor (T) for tallness or the factor (t) for shortness. Then, depending on whatever two sex cells fused to form a new individual, the resulting plant would either be tall, (TT) or (Tt), or short (tt). Again, because the factor for tallness (T) is dominant, any plant having that factor would be tall.

Mendel did other experiments in his monastery garden that threw even more light on how physical traits are passed along, or masked, in plants and animals from one generation to the next. And when his important work was rediscovered around the year 1900, the new science of heredity advanced rapidly. Two of the questions that were on the minds of biologists of the time were: If these "factors" of Mendel's were real, where were they to be found and how were they arranged?

Three

Chromosomes, Genes, and Sex

Mendel's inheritance laws turned out to be as sound for mice and humans as for the pea plants he grew in his monastery garden. Then why did his ideas go unappreciated for so long? One reason was that biologists were just beginning to gain important information about the nature of gametes, the details of fertilization, and how cells divide to produce new cells. Also, the importance of the cell nucleus was unfolding.

One cell divides into two new "daughter" cells in a process called mitosis, which takes about a d[...] in plant and animal cells. In a continuous series of stages, a substance called chromatin in the ce[...] nucleus develops into paired structures called chromosomes, which are the carriers of our genes. The chromosome pairs eventually break apart into two sets, one set going to each of the two ne[...] cells. This is the way our bodies make new cells for growth and to replace old cells.

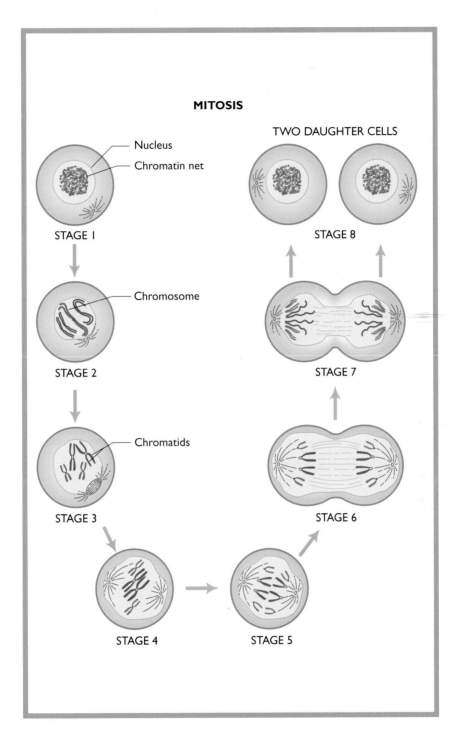

MITOSIS

Nucleus

Chromatin net

STAGE I

Chromosome

STAGE 2

Chromatids

STAGE 3

STAGE 4

STAGE 5

TWO DAUGHTER CELLS

STAGE 8

STAGE 7

STAGE 6

Hofmeister and Chromosomes

Almost twenty years before Mendel announced his findings, a German publisher became increasingly fascinated by what the microscope revealed about cell division. His name was Wilhelm Hofmeister. In 1848, at age twenty-four, he drew a sequence of diagrams showing that the nucleus of plant cells that produce pollen breaks down into smaller rod-shaped bodies as the cell prepares to divide. These bodies were later to be called *chromosomes*, from a Greek word meaning "colored bodies." They were given that name because they became highly visible when a dividing cell was stained with certain dyes. During that process of cell division, called *mitosis*, the cell nucleus can be seen to break down into two identical sets of chromosomes. One complete set goes to each of the two new "daughter" cells. Each of the new cells is just like the original parent cell.

Now we know that *every* form of life has a set number of chromosomes in its body cells. For instance, the fruit fly has 8,

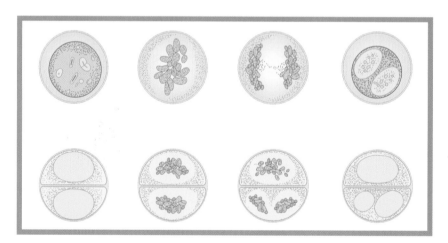

Wilhelm Hofmeister was among the first to actually watch a cell nucleus organize chromatin into chromosomes. Compare his sequence of sketches drawn in 1848 with the diagram on page 33.

the frog has 26, and people have 46. As opposed to ordinary body cells, when a sex cell divides into two new gametes, or sex cells, each of the two new cells receives only half the number of chromosomes. So each new human gamete ends up with only 23 chromosomes instead of 46. But during fertilization, when the sperm and egg cells fuse, the resulting offspring

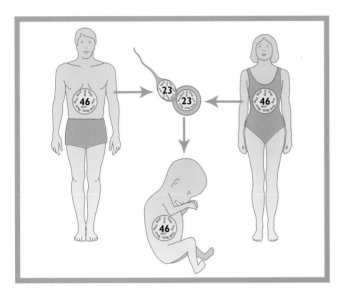

Each newborn child inherits one complete set of 46 chromosomes—23 from its mother's egg cell and 23 from its father's sperm cell.

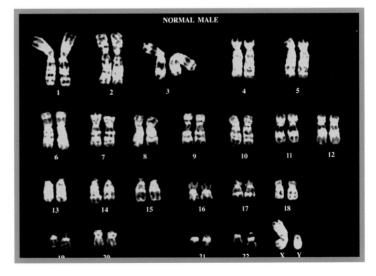

A normal human being has a total of forty-six chromosomes: twenty-two pairs of body chromosomes, called autosomes, plus a gender-identifying pair of chromosomes, XX for females and XY for males. This photo shows a male.

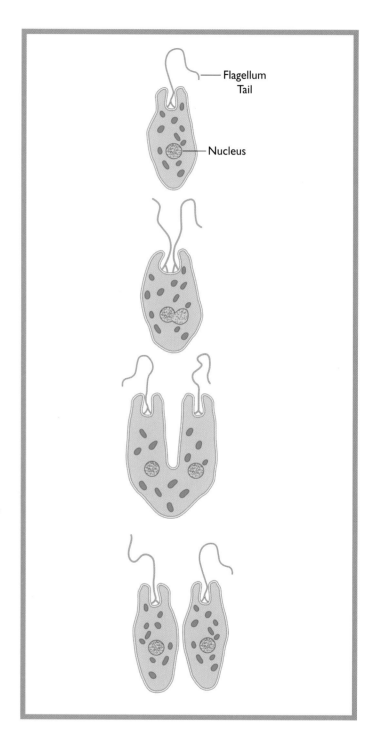

Euglena, *a single-cell organism, prepares for division by mitosis first by feeding and growing larger. A new whiplike tail forms as the nucleus begins to divide. The organism then splits lengthwise, one new nucleus and half the amount of remaining cell material moving into what will become two new daughter cells.*

inherits 46 chromosomes—23 from each parent. After fertilization, every new cell in the human infant receives a full set of 46 chromosomes.

Johannsen and Genes

It turned out that not even chromosomes were the illusive "factors" of inheritance imagined by Mendel. In 1902, a young geneticist at Columbia University named Walter S. Sutton reasoned that because there are far more heritable traits than there are chromosomes, each chromosome must be the carrier of many smaller units of inheritance. He was right.

During the first decade of the 1900s the Danish botanist Wilhelm Johannsen, like Mendel, experimented with plants. His work with bean plants showed that a plant's phenotype, or certain outward appearances such as seed size, could be affected by the plant's environment—soil type, soil nutrients, and amount of sunshine, for example. But some phenotype characteristics were handed down unchanged from one generation to the next. He called these unchanging characteristics *genotypes*. This distinction between phenotypes and genotypes was to give rise to the argument that goes on to this day. This argument asks, Which is more important, Nature or Nurture, heredity or the environment? By "environment," we include conditions of the mother's health and behavior while her child is still developing in the womb, and later the cultural and family influences on the child as it grows to adulthood.

Johannsen invented the term gene for those small chemical structures on the chromosomes. The forty-six chromosomes in humans turned out to have many thousands of genes. You can think of genes aligned along a chromosome like a string of birds perched on a telephone line. Each bird represents the position of an individual gene. The genotype, Johannsen said, was the sum of all of a person's genes combined. And he added that the phenotype was the sum of the genotype combined with environmental effects. It is important to remember that the environment within the mother's womb can determine whether the embryo will develop into a healthy child or one with physical or mental defects.

What Determines What Sex You Are?

Do you think you inherit your maleness or femaleness from your mother, your father, or both? And what is it that makes you male or female? By about 1900 biologists understood that a newborn's sex is established at the moment a sperm cell fertilizes an egg cell.

Of the twenty-three pairs of human chromosomes, a female has one pair of sex chromosomes identified as XX. A male also has a pair of sex chromosomes, but instead of having two X chromosomes the male has one X and one Y chromosome, written XY. Whenever a female sex cell divides into two new cells, each of the new cells receives an X chromosome. But when a male sex cell divides, one cell receives an

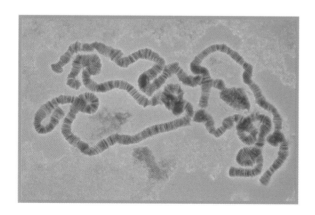

Giant chromosomes of a fruit fly. The one seen here is many, many times life size. It enabled biologists to study the chromosome's structure in detail. The light and darker bands correspond to certain traits.

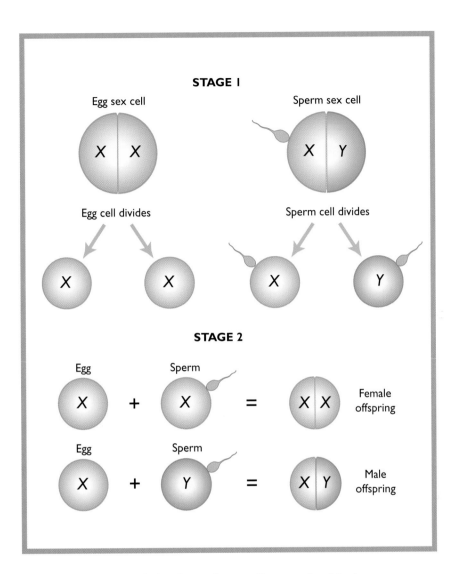

X chromosome while the other cell gets the Y chromosome. That means that there are two different kinds of sperm cells but only one kind of egg cell. Whether a newborn is to be a male or female depends on whether a Y sperm cell or an X sperm cell gets to fertilize the egg. So an egg fertilized by an X sperm ends up with an XX chromosome pair, which means the child will be female. An egg fertilized by a Y sperm ends up with an XY chromosome pair, which means the child will be male. Since a fertilized egg has about a fifty-fifty chance of having either an X sperm or Y sperm, there are just about as many men in the world as women.

Sex-linked Heredity

What other roles do the sex chromosomes play in our inheritance? For one thing, they determine genetic characteristics such as color blindness. Biologists say that such traits are sex-linked. In the early 1900s, the American geneticist Thomas Hunt Morgan did many experiments with fruit flies. One day he noticed that one collection of cultured flies included a fly with white eyes. Normally the eyes are red. After obtaining a strain of true-breeding white-eyed flies, Morgan did experiments showing that the white-eye trait was sex-linked. He crossed a red-eyed female fly that did not carry any genes for eye whiteness with a white-eyed male fly that carried a gene for eye whiteness on his X chromosome. The offspring all had red eyes, showing that red was dominant over white. (Recall that the offspring in Mendel's pea plant experiment were all tall plants, showing that tallness was dominant over shortness.) Further experiments showed that not only was the white-eyed trait recessive, but that it was sex-linked, since none of the female flies in the first generation ever had white eyes.

Geneticist Thomas Hunt Morgan established the relationship between genes and chromosomes. He and his co-workers were the first to develop gene maps showing the location of genes for various traits on different chromosomes.

Color blindness is another sex-linked hereditary trait. About 8 percent of white American males have it though only 1 percent of females do. Why? Because the gene for color blindness occurs on the male's X chromosome, not on the Y chromosome, a color-blind male passes on his color blindness only through his daughters. The trait is never passed on directly to his sons. Because females have two X chromosomes, they can carry the gene for color blindness but not have the disease. But because males have only one X chromosome, if that chromosome has the gene for color blindness, the male will be color blind. In other words, females have two chances of being normal for the characteristic while males have only one chance. This is also true for hemophilia, a disease caused by the blood's inability to clot and so stop bleeding. A hemophiliac can die from a simple cut or pulled tooth.

It turns out that males of any population stand a greater chance of inheriting any sex-linked trait than females.

Such is the nature of science and of human curiosity, that every time a question about genetics was answered, a new one arose. Among them was how a trait just seemed to come out of thin air. Another was why everyone was not the same; why, for example, there were differences in height, hair color, and size in a population.

A gene mutation in England's Queen Victoria apparently started the bleeding disease called hemophilia in the British royal family and, due to intermarriage, other European royal families. Queen Victoria did not have the disease but carried it genetically. It affected one of her four sons. Two of her daughters carried the gene into the Russian and Spanish royal families. Hemophilia usually only affects males. They inherit the disease only from their mothers.

Four

Mutations and Variation

Imagine a society in which all human beings are alike. All are the same height, have the same blood type, have blue eyes and blond hair, and six fingers on each hand. Their dogs are all English setters with exactly the same brown and white markings because that is the only breed of dog. It is a society of individuals lacking what biologists term variation. Things usually are much livelier and more interesting when the many different traits get all mixed up to produce individual people, dogs, and other organisms that are different from one another in many ways. Sometimes, however, the differences can turn out to be unwanted, grotesque, and even deadly. What causes all of these variations?

Sometimes, mutations can be good, but usually the change is a bad one. The hind legs of these frogs have been deformed as a result of mutation.

Mutations and Change

When genes get changed by being shifted around on a chromosome or exposed to radiation or certain harmful chemicals, the change is called a *mutation*, and mutations can change us in many different ways. Sometimes the change can be to our advantage, but almost always it is for the worse.

Things do not always go well when chromosomes split while preparing for cell division. Instead of splitting cleanly, the two may get tangled and wrap around each other. When they do finally separate, each new chromosome may break away with an exchanged assortment of genes. For instance, a chromosome with one gene for blond hair and one for blue eyes may exchange with its twin chromosome the part containing the gene for blond hair and receive in exchange a part containing a gene for brown hair. Now suppose that one of

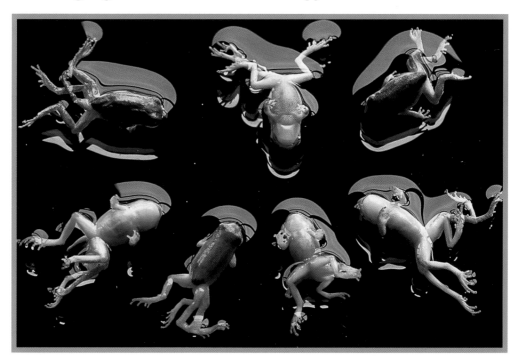

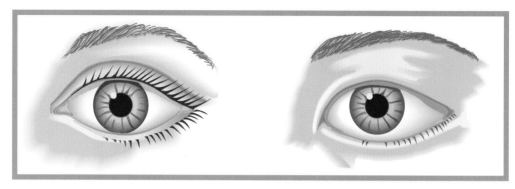

The eyes of an Asian person have curved, overlapping eyelids compared with those of a Caucasian. Both eye types are determined by genes inherited from an offspring's parents.

the crossed-over chromosomes becomes part of a sperm cell and the other one becomes part of an egg cell. When the chromosomes pair during fertilization, the resulting offspring will inherit an unusual gene combination for blue eyes and brown hair. Blond hair and blue eyes almost always go together because the genes for them are linked to one another. But if there is a mistake made during crossing-over of two chromosomes, the genes become unlinked and produce a blue-eyed person with brown instead of blond hair.

Crossing-over of chromosomes is only one way mutations are formed. Exposure to X rays can damage or otherwise change genes. That is why when you have your teeth X-rayed, the dentist always puts a lightweight lead shield over your body and then stands behind a lead shield. Exposure to certain chemicals can also cause mutations. Another source that has caused concern is the radiation in waste materials from nuclear power plants and the radiation released by nuclear weapons dumps. Mutations also occur when a sex cell receives the wrong number of chromosomes. For example, if a male cell gains an extra X chromosome and becomes XXY instead of the normal XY type, the male offspring will have small testes, not much body hair, and enlarged breasts. The lack of one X chromosome in a female, giving her an XO genotype instead of the normal XX, results in a woman having low-set ears, a webbed neck, underdeveloped breasts, and other abnormal conditions. If the chromosome appears as a triplet rather than a double, the child will be born with a condition called Down syndrome, meaning abnormal facial features and mental retardation. People with Down syndrome usually die before age thirty.

Once biologists found out how genes are arranged on chromosomes, they were able to draw up genetic maps for certain animals. They also learned to predict how often certain mutations occur. For instance, in humans, the mutation causing a person to be a dwarf occurs in forty-one out of one million gametes, or sex cells. The mutation for complete color blindness occurs in twenty-eight of every one million gametes. It now seems that perhaps one out of every one hundred

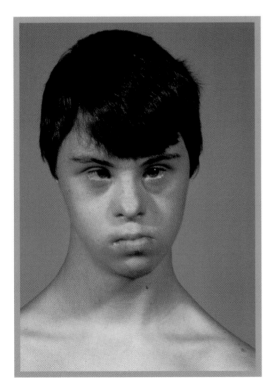

People with Down syndrome are almost always mentally retarded, have an atypical eye fold structure, a short and stocky body, and a thick neck. The birth defect is caused by having three instead of two chromosomes as pair number 21 (see chromosome illustration on page 35).

gametes carries a new mutation. These, then, are the raw materials of variation in a population.

So far, we have been talking about genes as if they were tiny chemical lumps forever fixed to chromosome strands. But what are these lumps made of? In 1953 biologists James Watson and Francis Crick finally solved the puzzle. They showed that genes have the form of a double spiral, giant molecule comprised

James Watson (left) and Francis Crick made biological history in 1953 when they discovered the complex structure of DNA molecules. Genes, for so long mystery structures, turned out to be DNA.

of deoxyribonucleic acid, or DNA. Each gene, then, can be thought of as a small chemical factory that helps influence what we look like and how we behave.

Also in the 1950s, a group of French biologists showed that genes are not forever nailed in place to chromosomes. They spoke of "free-floating" genetic material called episomes and plasmids that they found in bacteria. Later, other scientists discovered such free-floating material in higher organisms. Still later, biologists observed free-floating genes in those cell structures known as mitochondria and chloroplasts. The genes of those cell structures are inherited separately from the genes on chromosomes. It now seems that there are even genes within genes. By 1980 biologists were convinced that certain genes commonly move around inside a chromosome, from one chromosome to another, and from one organism to another. They are called jumping DNA. Bacteria have the knack of exchanging sections of their DNA with one another. Because bacteria reproduce so rapidly—once every twenty minutes or so—and because they can easily swap DNA segments, they quickly "learn" to resist antibiotics as fast as scientists create new ones. That is one reason why disease-causing germs spread so rapidly.

A major international scientific undertaking called the Human Genome Project began in 1990. It has taken on the gigantic task of mapping every human gene, of which there are from 30,000 to 40,000. Over the years to come, the project will reap fantastic benefits for humans. Detailed knowledge about DNA will provide new ways to diagnose, treat, and someday prevent thousands of disorders that affect us. The project is likely to have still other benefits that we cannot even predict.

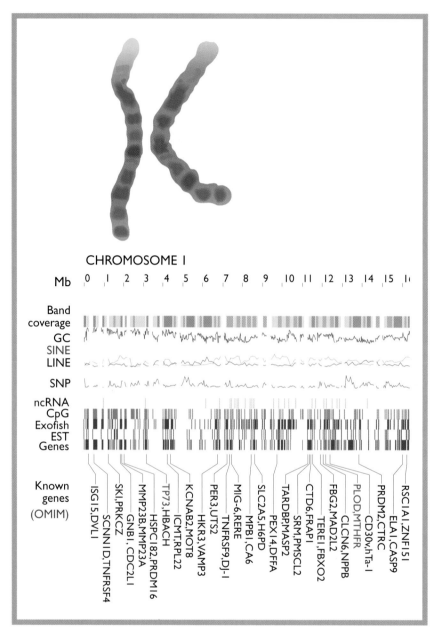

Human chromosome number 1 shows the location of many genes. Gene mapping has been going on since 1990 in an effort to map the location of every human gene as part of an international study sponsored by the United States called the Human Genome Project.

Sickle-Cell Anemia

This dreaded disease, common among African blacks, but less common among American blacks, is an interesting example of a mutation that can be advantageous to some but deadly to others.

Sickle-cell anemia is a mutation that changes the shape of red blood cells from an oval to a sickle shape. The abnormal cells tend to rupture, which causes anemia, or a shortage of red blood cells. The crescent-shaped cells also get clogged in the small blood vessels. There are two genotypes for the disease. One person may have one dominant gene and one recessive gene for the disease, written (Aa). Or a person may have two recessive genes, (aa), which means that the person is almost certain to die before reaching childbearing age. An (Aa) genotype person, however, nearly always survives and has only mild anemia.

The sickling gene is common in tropical Africa, with as many as 40 percent of some communities having the trait. How can so many individuals carry the trait when so many (aa) genotypes die before they can pass the condition on to the next generation? It turns out that there is an advantage to carrying the trait. Around 1950 investigators discovered that most people with the sickling gene lived in areas where malaria is widespread. They also found that those people rarely came down with malaria. So the sickling gene enabled children with the trait to escape death by malaria. As adults they then passed the trait on to their offspring. In that way the gene was kept alive and well in the gene pool of the local community. A gene pool is the total collection of genes in a population.

Investigators then reasoned that in areas where malaria was not a threat, the sickle-cell trait probably would be less common.

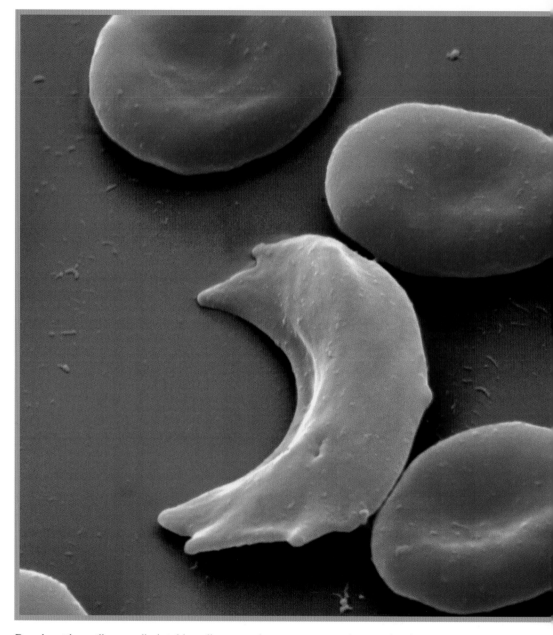

People with an illness called sickle-cell anemia have a mixture of normal red blood cells (oval disks) with deformed red cells shaped like a sickle. The sickle cells rupture and die, leaving a person with fewer and fewer red blood cells. The condition, called anemia, virtually always leads to early death.

It turned out that only about 8 percent of black Americans living in the United States, where malaria was rare, had the trait. Since the genotype had no advantage among American blacks, the sickling gene tended to become lost.

"Monsters" of Heredity

Every thirty seconds somewhere in the world a child is born deformed. Such abnormalities have shocked and fascinated people for thousands of years. Every now and then a child is born with two heads, with a single eye in the middle of its forehead, or without arms. There are many lesser deformities. A newborn might have six instead of five fingers or never reach full height and become a dwarf.

During the Middle Ages, from about 900 to 1500, magic, witchcraft, and superstition dominated people's thinking. Women often were burned at the stake for the "crime" of giving birth to deformed infants. Often the infants were thrown into rivers or left to perish in the wild. The practice, called infanticide, was done quite openly, without shame, and without punishment. It was probably done out of a feeling of frustration and helplessness in not being

Dwarfism is caused by genetic mutation. Regarded with amusement in the middle ages, dwarfs often served as court jesters, as in this painting by Spanish artist Diego Velasquez entitled The Jester, Sebastian de Morra.

The idea of mythical beings—or animals with human qualities—lasted into early Christian times. The unicorn, part of Christian mythology, was associated with the Virgin Mary and Jesus Christ.

able to prevent such misfortunes. Dwarfs, on the other hand, were regarded with amusement and were often permitted to appear in the courts of kings as clowns.

There also were fanciful stories about women having children by a goat, a dog, or other animals. The resulting "monsters" were half-human creatures. Many ancient stone carvings from Mesopotamia and the Nile Valley of Egypt show double-headed or part-human, part-animal creatures. Such deformed beings were often said to be the work of angry gods and were possessed of evil spirits. Others, such as mythical beings that were half-human and half-lion, for example, were admired for their combination of two great strengths.

The Environment and Deformity

As early as the mid-1800s medical investigators became aware that certain changes in the environment of a developing embryo could cause deformities. The French biologist Étienne Geoffroy Saint-Hilaire, who lived from 1772 to 1844, found that if he varnished the air pores in the shell of a hen's egg, the chicks were born deformed because they did not get enough oxygen before hatching. One experimenter created sea urchins with two heads by allowing the embryos to develop in excessively warm water. Another produced one-eyed fish by raising the embryos in water with more than the usual amount of salt.

So it soon became clear that the environment of a developing embryo could cause abnormalities. Humans were no exception. In 1957 a German pharmaceutical firm introduced a new sleeping pill, thalidomide. The drug was sold for four years in forty countries to many people, including pregnant women. Though marketed as "absolutely safe," thalidomide had not been tested for side effects or safe use by pregnant

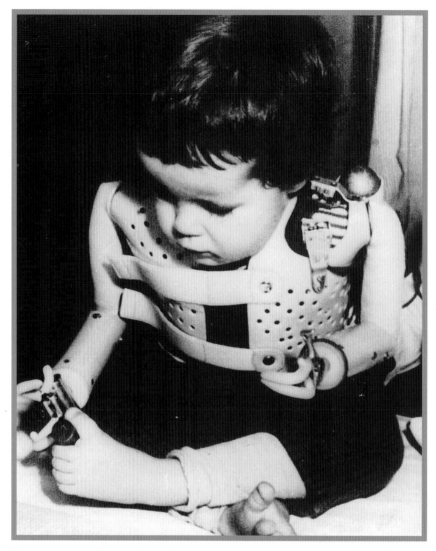

Drugs are not always "miracle cures," as many pregnant women found to their horror when they used the sleeping pill thalidomide, which began to be prescribed in the late 1950s. Like this little girl, many babies were born without arms or functional legs. The use of the drug was discontinued in the early 1960s.

women. Its dangers soon loomed large. In 1959 many babies were born without arms, or with small flippers instead of arms.

Other infants were born without legs or with stumps instead of legs. By 1961 still more "thalidomide babies" had been born. In only a few months 154 deformed infants were delivered in one West German hospital. By late 1961 about 6,000 infants were deformed by the drug worldwide.

By the end of that year, a German physician had tracked down thalidomide as the culprit. Mothers of the affected infants all had taken the drug during that stage when their embryos were developing arms and legs. Although the German physician did not name the drug when he reported his findings, other German doctors suspected it was thalidomide and immediately stopped using the drug. Halfway around the world, an Australian physician sounded the alarm by implicating thalidomide by name. By the end of November, the drug had been taken off the market in Germany. Through the good work of Dr. Frances O. Kelsey, of the U.S. Food and Drug Administration, the sale of thalidomide in the United States was never authorized, so its widespread use was blocked. Nevertheless, some pregnant women managed to get the drug from Europe. Of the 6,000 known thalidomide babies, some died, others were put to death, and most of the rest have learned to function with the aid of artificial limbs.

The sad lesson was driven home to young women who were pregnant or planning to have babies in the future. Avoid antibiotics, alcohol, sedatives, and other drugs that can affect the chemical environment of the womb and the well-being of a developing embryo. Even without drugs, many things can go wrong in a pregnancy. All a mother can do is take the best care possible to ensure she doesn't do anything that might lead to birth defects in her offspring.

Five

Race, Racism, and Genes

All humans are members of the species *Homo sapiens sapiens*. There are no other human species, although there are various geographical races of modern humans.

The Origin of Human Races

A race within any species can be thought of as a group of populations that have certain genes and physical characteristics in common. Those characteristics then set that group of populations apart from all other populations of the same species. As *Homo sapiens sapiens,* people increased their numbers and populated virtually every part of the world by about 50,000 years ago, their various populations gradually adapted to different regional environments and so evolved geographical races.

Abnormally short fingers and hands, a condition known as brachydactyly, which is shown here, is an example of a dominant defect that can be passed on from parent to offspring through many generations. More severe deformities usually are not passed on because the individual is unable to reproduce offspring.

Populations of all organisms ebb and flow and change in response to changes in the environment, and they have done so throughout the history of life on this planet. Human populations are no exception. Their genes are subject to environmental pressures, as are the genes of other species. This is why human populations living in markedly different environments have adapted differently. For example, the Eskimos' relatively short fingers are thought to be an adaptation to a cold environment. Short fingers have less surface area from which to lose heat than do long fingers, so short fingers tend to lessen the risk of frostbite. On the other hand, people adapted to a hot climate tend to have long limbs, an adaptation that promotes heat loss and so prevents overheating of the body. Indians living in the Andes mountains of South America have evolved relatively

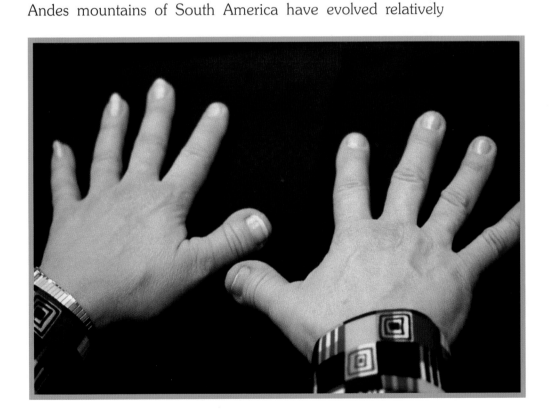

People's physical characteristics differ for many reasons, but we are all part of the same human family—one that has become increasingly global due to intermarriage over many centuries of civilization.

large chests with larger lungs and a larger supply of blood than people living at sea level. These features are adaptations to life at high altitude, where oxygen is harder to come by because of the lower atmospheric pressure.

The dark skin of native Africans may be an ancient adaptation that protected the skin from the damaging action of ultraviolet radiation, which is more intense near the Equator than in middle and high latitudes. Dark skin is caused by a coloring substance called melanin. All people have some melanin in their skin, but native Africans, Australian Aborigines, and people of Dravidian ancestry in India have more of it than do Chinese, Japanese, or Norwegians. Skin with lots of melanin may have been favored and passed on genetically because it protected against damaging radiation from the Sun. But in high latitudes, such as northern Europe, dark skin would not have been an advantage because large amounts of melanin interfere with vitamin D production in the skin through the action of sunlight. So the adaptation of a light skin color with small amounts of melanin would have been favored and handed down genetically in Scandinavians.

You sometimes hear people speak of the "Italian race" or the "Jewish race." There is, of course, no such thing. There is a Jewish religion or a Catholic religion, people of Italian nationality or French nationality, but none of these is a *race*. And the fact that people of some groups, such as Jews, have a number of genetic traits in common does not make them a race. For example, nine out of ten infants born with a fatal disease known as Tay-Sachs are Jewish, most of northeastern European origin. But others born with the disease are not Jewish just because they are born with the disease. People are Jewish if they practice the religion or are born to Jewish parents.

You also sometimes hear of the "Aryan race," though no such race exists. Aryans are people who speak languages that are offshoots of the Indo-European root language. Such languages include German, Italian, French, and English. An Aryan is any native speaker of one of those languages. More than a century ago certain Germans believed in something called pan-Germanism. It was a notion that peoples who spoke any of the languages related to German were superior to all others and were destined to rule all other "inferior races." And the Russians preached pan-Slavism, the idea that all Slavic-speaking peoples were the true superior race. But these are cultural groups, not races. And the idea of superiority was, of course, pure propoganda.

Are You a Racist?

The belief that people can be grouped not only into races, but races that are inferior or superior, is called *racism*. Racism is as old as the hills and every bit as alive today as it was thousands of years ago. And it is not likely to go away soon.

The basis of racism is the belief that certain groups mistakenly called "races"—American, Inuit, Chinese, or English, for instance—are born with differences in mind and body that make one group superior and another inferior. For example, the fact that most American blacks are descended from slaves was once at the root of much of the bias against blacks and promoted the belief that blacks were inferior. Those who persist in that belief point to national test scores that so often show black children's scores significantly lower than those of whites or Chinese. But all so-called racial groups seem to have about the same number of intelligent individuals. It is their cultural and economic backgrounds that can create differences. Our present knowledge of genetics indicates that anyone who believes in racial superiority is either ignorant or misguided.

The Nazis who ruled Germany from 1933 to 1945 were extreme racists. Acting on their beliefs, they murdered six million Jews before and during World War II. They also killed 5 million others they believed to be inferior. They were convinced that the people of northwestern Europe, and especially Germany, were members of what they called the *Herrenvolk*, which means "master race." They looked down on the Poles, Russians, and especially the Jews as inferior races. They thought that every Pole, Russian, or Jew inherited

Although racism continues to limit achievement among minority groups, an increasing number of minority individuals of exceptional achievement continue to win appointments to high positions in government and industry, such as Condaleeza Rice, national security adviser to President George W. Bush.

inferiority from birth and so would always remain inferior, no matter what his or her achievements in life. In many countries Jews could not own land. In Germany at that time, they were barred from military or civil service. Having one Jewish grandparent was enough to brand a person inferior and have him packed off to a concentration camp.

Today in the United States racism is a common attitude and is directed against not only groups, but individuals. We see it in *racial profiling* whenever a black, a Hispanic, or an Arab is stopped by the police not because he has broken the law but because of his appearance. In the early 1900s when the floodgates of immigration were opened in this country, people by the thousands poured in and settled in their own little communities. Many were Italian, Dutch, German, Irish, and Chinese. They were resented largely because they spoke different languages, came from unfamiliar cultures, and kept to themselves, often because they were not encouraged to become part of mainstream America. Later there was an influx of Japanese, and today we have communities of Vietnamese, Cambodians, Thai, and many others. New York and San Francisco have their Chinatowns. Florida and California have rapidly growing populations of Hispanics and Latinos.

Many immigrants believe they are criticized no matter what they do. They feel they are resented if they stay within their own group and do not learn to speak English, but they often meet hostility if they try to mix into the mainstream culture. Often racial slurs and

In the name of extreme racism, six million Jews were killed by the German Nazi Party during World War II. The Nazis justified their actions by the belief that the Jews were a lesser race that, if allowed to remain alive, would continue to pass down their inferior genes throughout the generations, therefore diminishing the achievements of the human race. In fact, some of the "lesser" Jews throughout history have included the Nobel Prize-winning physicist Albert Einstein, who managed to escape the Nazis, the Pulitzer-Prize-winning novelist Philip Roth, and achievers in every field too numerous to count.

other racist expressions come out when the majority culture, or some part of it, feels threatened.

Geographic Races

The idea that the modern human geographical races have evolved as a result of population adaptations over thousands of years is hard to challenge, even if some of the causes are not yet clear. Over thousands of years different human populations have gone slightly but significantly separate ways to avoid a harsh environment or in search of a still better one. In response to changing environmental conditions, peoples of tens of thousands of years ago wandered to different parts of the world, and their populations became products of their environments. And so the geographic races evolved, each providing its local gene pool with DNA that would come to distinguish geographical groups from one another. But those distinct geographical groups have not remained unchanged. Groups have always mixed through intermarriage, with the results of sharing and enrichments of gene pools.

There is no such thing as a "pure race," meaning one that forever remains the same. Because all humans belong to the same species, our various populations are capable of interbreeding, and interbreeding has been the rule throughout human history. Time and again, as invaders of one geographical race have conquered a neighboring people, the populations have mixed and their racial distinctions have blurred slightly. As biologist E. Peter Volpe has remarked, "The whole world today is a single large neighborhood. Modern man lives in one great reproductive community."

Races, then, are little more than temporary collections of genes in a population's gene pool. They are just temporary and passing stages in the ever-changing history of our, or any other, species.

Six

Genes in Our Future

Ever since people learned to cultivate plants and domesticate animals some ten thousand years ago, they have experimented to bring about changes to suit their needs, or sometimes their desires. Originally, they did so by unknowingly manipulating genes to steer hereditary traits one way or another. These attempts were the first experiments in what is called *genetic engineering*.

Fixing Bad Genes

The results of early experiments in breeding are numerous and include many decorative and edible plants, the Great Dane dog, the toylike Shetland pony, and the elegant Arabian show horse. Today we are more skilled than the plant and animal breeders of earlier times, and our experimenting is much more finely tuned. We are now developing the ability to redesign ourselves by fixing hereditary defects

Over many centuries, animal breeders have selected individuals with prized traits to produce the perfect cat, the handsomest dog, the fastest horse, or the fattest hog. Among the products of controlled breeding are unusual varieties such as a miniature horse only 32 inches (81 cm) high, a Great Dane, and a miniature Schnauzer.

that have haunted people for ages—hemophilia and sickle-cell anemia among them. We are on the verge of producing tailor-made genes.

The first possibility of genetic engineering came in 1968 when the Nobel Prize winner Arthur Kornberg and his associates made an artificial copy of the DNA of a virus. That breakthrough led to the possibility of creating harmless ready-made viruses that contain tailor-made genes. Such a virus could then be injected into the liver, or some other organ, that had crippling defective genes. The healthy tailor-made genes would then go to work and produce certain chemicals (enzymes), the lack of which caused the genetic disorder. Researchers are now looking forward to the day when surgery with laser beams might cut out or repair defective segments of DNA.

What happens if we can't fix a genetic disorder? In the case of gross physical disorders, such as a two-headed baby or twins whose bodies are joined together at birth, the individuals usually die soon after birth. People born with severe mental disorders may have to be cared for in special institutions. But what about people with lesser disabilities that are painful to see,

American biochemist Arthur Kornberg and his associates paved the way for genetic engineering and the possibility that it might correct some disabling genetic disorders, such as sickle-cell anemia.

When a fertilized egg divides imperfectly, the result can be Siamese twins, two individuals joined at the abdomen, chest or back, for example. In some cases they can be separated surgically just after birth. In other instances, such as these girls joined at the torso, the separation may be extremely difficult or even impossible.

and that are likely to be passed on to a future generation if that person has children? Some say the only way to solve the problem is to prevent "unfit" people from having children. Their bad genes would then not be passed on. This notion is called *eugenics.* To eliminate a genetic disorder from a population by controlled breeding could take up to two thousand years. Furthermore, by preventing such people from contributing their bad genes to their population's gene pool, you would also prevent them from contributing any exceptionally good genes. The Nazi's program of breeding blond-haired, blue-eyed members of their mythical master race was also part of a eugenics movement.

Clones: Dolly, Polly, and You

In 1997 biologists in Scotland surprised the scientific community by announcing that they had "made," or *cloned,* a sheep. This sheep, named Dolly, was identical to her mother. Then came another cloned sheep named Polly, and then a homemade calf named Gene.

More recently, researchers in Hawaii have cloned mice and then made a second and third generation of clones, all the animals being genetically identical. They did it by first removing the nucleus of an adult mouse cell and then injecting it into an egg cell from which its nucleus had been removed. Cytoplasm of the egg cell then somehow chemically activated the genes contained in the nucleus of the implanted adult cell. The egg then developed into a healthy embryo, which became a healthy mouse, normal in every way except that it didn't have, or need, a father to help it into the world.

While scientists generally cheer such cloning events for what they teach us about how organisms develop, some religious groups do not approve of such experimentation for fear that it will one day lead to cloning human beings. Some governments, including the United States, have banned all experimentation in human cloning because they regard it as "tampering with human life." Some scientists feel that it is now possible to take a few of your body cells and genetically engineer them to produce a duplicate of yourself. Such a notion bothers some people who imagine a science-fiction army of cloned human beings, all identical, at the control of one authority figure. Such an idea is pretty far-fetched. Suppose that you were cloned and had a cloned twin. Further suppose that your clone twin were adopted and raised by different parents, educated differently from you, brought up in a

Sheep clones Megan and Morgan, produced in the laboratory at the Roslin Institute in Edinburgh, Scotland. Which is which makes no difference since the two are exactly alike, the products of manipulating the development of identical embryonic cells.

different country, and taught to speak a different language. Your home environment would mold you into an individual rather different from that of your clone twin.

The Nobel Prize–winner Marshall W. Nirenberg once cautioned, "When man becomes capable of instructing his own cells, he must refrain from doing so until he has sufficient wisdom to use this knowledge for the benefit of mankind." But can people ever reach a stage when they have "sufficient knowledge," or a sufficiently high sense of morality, to do only "the right thing"? And who is to determine what the right thing is? Was unleashing the power of the atom to produce first atomic, and then nuclear, explosives doing the right thing? But what about nuclear power plants? others ask. Aren't they a good thing? Some answer no, saying that they are as potentially dangerous as nuclear weapons because of the long-lived deadly radiation wastes they introduce into the environment. Those wastes, as is well known, increase the number of mutations. And since nearly all mutations are genetic changes for the worse, the dangers from radioactive wastes are very real.

However, it is hard to point to a time when any scientific development was stopped in its tracks for long because of political, religious, ethical, or moral reasons. And it is highly unlikely that experiments in genetic engineering involving human beings will ever be stopped. Once a new scientific development breaks through wherever there is freedom of thought, there is no stopping it or turning back.

Acquired characteristics—any of an organism's characteristics that were not inherited genetically.

Blending inheritance—an early, but false, notion that if an animal with black fur mated with a similar animal with white fur, all of the offspring would have gray fur, and that the original black-fur and white-fur traits would be lost because, once blended, the two traits could never be separated again.

Cytoplasm—a fluid that is part of a biological cell.

Embryo—the developmental stage of a new individual from a zygote.

Eugenics—a movement devoted to "improving" the human species through control of heredity factors in mating.

Fertilization—the union of a male and female cell.

Gamete—a sex cell, such as a sperm cell or ovum (egg cell).

Gene—a chemical structure called DNA that is responsible for the transmission of traits from parent to offspring.

Genetic engineering—the science of manipulating genes to bring about changes in a genotype or phenotype.

Genetics—the study of the composition and actions of genes and their role in inheritance.

Genotype—genetic makeup of an individual.

Heredity—the study of how traits are passed on by parents to offspring.

Homunculus—a miniature of a completely formed individual once believed to be contained in the head of a sperm cell.

Mitosis—the process by which a cell nucleus divides and gives rise to two daughter cells with the same number of chromosomes as the original cell nucleus.

Mutation—any change in a gene, usually for the worse.

Nucleus—the control center of a biological cell.

Pangenesis—an old belief that all parts of the body contributed some genetic materials, or essence, to heredity and that all were then collected in the male and female.

Phenotype—physical character or appearance.

Racism—the belief that people can be grouped into races that are inferior or superior.

Spontaneous generation—an old belief that living organisms were created out of nonliving matter, such as Aristotle's belief that fireflies were produced from dew.

Zygote—a fertilized egg, resulting from the union of an egg cell and a sperm cell.

Boyd, William C., and Isaac Asimov. *Races and People*. New York: Abelard-Schuman, 1955.

Comfort, Nathaniel C. "Are Genes Real?" *Natural History*. June 2001, pp. 28–44.

Darlington, C. D. *Genetics and Man*. New York: Macmillan, 1964.

Dobzhansky, Theodosium. *Genetic Diversity and Human Equality*. New York: Basic Books, 1973.

Gallant, Roy A. *Before the Sun Dies: The Story of Evolution*. New York: Macmillan, 1989.

Kalmus, H. *Genetics*. Garden City, NY: Doubleday, 1964.

McKusick, Victor A. *Human Genetics, 2nd ed.* Englewood Cliffs, NJ: Prentice-Hall, 1969.

Volpe, E. Peter. *Human Heredity and Birth Defects*. New York: Pegasus, 1971.

Index

Page numbers for illustrations are in **boldface**.

About the Author

Roy A. Gallant, called "one of the deans of American science writers for children" by *School Library Journal*, is the author of almost one hundred books on scientific subjects, including the National Geographic Society's *Atlas of Our Universe*. Among his other books are *When the Sun Dies*; *Earth: The Making of a Planet*; *Before the Sun Dies*; *Earth's Vanishing Forests*; *The Day the Sky Split Apart*, which won the 1997 John Burroughs award for nature writing; and *Meteorite Hunting*, a collection of accounts about his expeditions to Siberia to document major meteorite impact crater events. His most recent award is a lifetime achievement award presented to him by the Maine Library Association.

From 1979 to 2000, (professor emeritus) Gallant was director of the Southworth Planetarium at the University of Southern Maine. He has taught astronomy there and at the Maine College of Art. For several years he was on the staff of New York's American Museum of Natural History and a member of the faculty of the museum's Hayden Planetarium. His specialty is documenting on film and in writing the history of major Siberian meterorite impact sites. To date, he has organized eight expeditions to Russia and is planning his ninth, which will take him into the Altai Mountains near Mongolia. He has written articles about his expeditions for *Sky & Telescope* magazine and for the journal *Meteorite*. Professor Gallant is a fellow of the Royal Astronomical Society of London and a member of the New York Academy of Sciences. He lives in Rangeley, Maine.